fritz henle's rollei

# fritz henle's rollei

## PHOTOGRAPHS BY FRITZ HENLE

WITH TEXT BY VIVIENNE TALLAL WINTERRY

HASTINGS HOUSE    PUBLISHERS    NEW YORK

Jacket, Layout, Typography by
ROBERT FABIAN

fritz henle's rollei

# FOREWORD

This book represents to me more than a document of twenty years of my work in photography and, in particular, my work with the Rolleiflex, the camera that seems to respond most readily to my touch. Like the fine tools of the other visual arts, my camera is only my tool for expressing myself.

The pictures here have not been arranged in chronological or geographical sequence, but only according to the patterns or ideas they suggest. When you look at them, one by one, you will know that the technical process which brought them into being has always been secondary to the emotional attitude in which they were conceived. In them there is grief and laughter, strength and weakness, happiness and despair, love and hate—but how can I hope to encompass all this in a mere hundred pages of photographs?

These pictures, then, are the result of a search—a search through which all my visions have been crystallized into images on film. In these images is the expression of my love of life in all its variety.

F. H.

**F**RITZ HENLE'S camera extracts the essence of a moment. Fleeting laughter, the swirl of a skirt, the significant pattern of inanimate objects, the real character of a place—all are captured with a click of the Rollei's shutter.

Henle is an exponent of photographic naturalism, and his insistence on the integrity of his subject is mirrored in everything he does. Background must contribute its share of meaning to the photograph; lighting, wherever possible, must be limited to that which is naturally present; a human model must show no trace of self-consciousness or camera-consciousness.

Henle's way with his Rolleiflex is so utterly uncomplicated that there appears to be nothing to it that you or I or the neighbor's little boy couldn't do as well. But his effortlessness is deceptive; it is a by-product of his complete mastery of the instrument. Behind the consummate skill with which he operates the camera lie years of training, of self-discipline, of exploring the potentialities and limitations of this compact mechanism with which he works.

Years of intensive and widely-varied picture-making experience have led Henle to regard the Rollei as a part of himself. It is an extension of his imagination, of his visualization. It is a sensitively obedient servant in his capable hands.

In his youth, Fritz Henle attended the School of Photography in Munich. Here, photography was stubbornly regarded as a craft, and students were trained first of all in the principles of faithful reproduction of subject matter, and provided with a thorough fundamental knowledge of photographic chemistry. For nearly two years he studied, struggling for self-expression in an atmosphere which did not encourage artistic imagination. He yearned to record on film the personalities of his classmates, the spirit of their gay comradeship, and the subtle and intricate variations, more sensed than seen, in the features of the students who came there from every corner of the earth.

He wanted to convey, as in a quick glance, the mood of a spring evening; to capture the drama of an instant. The poetry of light playing on stone especially demanded expression through his lens. Yet each time he maneuvered his clumsy equipment into position and pulled the black cloth over his head, he knew he had lost the spontaneity of the composition as his mind's eye had conceived it.

Photographs emerged from his darkroom beautifully correct in perspective, clear in detail, but—lifeless. Only young Fritz's determination kept him at it.

In 1931, when he was about to receive his diploma, an incident occurred which was ultimately to release him from bondage to the cumbersome equipment with which he was impatient, and make possible the living photographs he had dreamed of making. Idle curiosity made him pause to examine an early-model Rolleiflex displayed in a store window. Its compactness and simplicity of operation appealed to him strongly. These very characteristics, along with its small negative size, had caused it to be considered inadequate for the serious photographer.

Twenty years of respectful obedience to parents and teachers had not dimmed his willingness to accept a new idea, even though it might be unacceptable to established authority. Now he was determined to own this camera which would allow him at last to move about freely, which would give him a faithful right-side-up image of his subject, and which, by its uncomplicated mechanism, would permit him to bring spontaneity to his pictures. The tiresome and forbidding aspects of photography would be eliminated, and both he and his subject could bring a natural freshness to the finished product.

He felt strongly that he must own the Rolleiflex, in spite of the disdain exhibited by those who were used to larger cameras. Only one small consideration stood in the way of his purchase: he had no money.

So, for a time, he had to continue as before. He tried to express his delight in the ripple of water, but his result came no nearer what he wanted than the resemblance of a stuffed lark to a bird in flight. He turned instead to the story to be found in rocks and stones. If the flash of sun on water, or the smile on a girl's lips would not respect the limitations of his inadequate equipment, then at least the stones, the great granite rocks would allow him to record their patterns and their meanings.

He photographed the great concrete mass of the locks at Bremerhaven, and his pictures came to the attention of an official of the North German Lloyd Steamship Lines. Not aware that Henle was a student, the official sent him a letter offering him an immediate 30-day job on a Mediterranean cruise, making pictures to promote travel.

He did not hesitate, though he knew he was enrolled in a school whose nineteenth-century traditions prescribed expulsion and disgrace for a breach of discipline. Knowing, too, that without a diploma a job might be hard to find, he wrote his acceptance to the steamship company. By the same mail, he wrote to the school, saying that he had been called home but would return as soon as possible to make up the work he missed, so that he might graduate with his class.

Here was a way to acquire the money for the Rolleiflex! He had hoped to remain anonymous, but he did not reckon with the enterprise of the steamship company's publicity department. His pictures of Egyptian pyramids, Moorish arches, and Turkish minarets were well received, and displayed in travel offices all over the country — Munich included.

The truant was back in school, stirring up plenty of interest with his new Rolleiflex. Then, one Sunday, there appeared in the rotogravure section of the local paper a magnificent study of a pyramid, bearing the credit line "Fritz Henle." Storms raged in the school director's private office. Only the intervention of a sympathetic teacher saved Henle from disgrace. She pointed out to the indignant faculty that the school's aim was to produce competent photographers, and that if they had succeeded so well with one student that he had prematurely outgrown his amateur status — so much more credit to him, and to the school which produced him.

Fritz was relieved to be let off so lightly, for the completion of his course was important to him. Now, at last, he had found himself, and his future lay before him.

His eloquent study of a pyramid which had caused such a tempest came to the attention of Prof. Clarence Kennedy, an art historian from Smith College, who was working in Florence on a special project, with a Guggenheim Fellowship. He offered Henle a job as his assistant. Here was a chance to live and work in one of the most beautiful lands on earth. Fritz telephoned his acceptance, and left on the next train for Florence.

Young, eager, and impressionable, he absorbed the sunlight, the laughter and the language of Italy; her arts were his lessons. He learned composition, form, balance, the distribution of parts within an artistic whole. The esthetic lessons of these early years in Italy are fundamental to the development of Henle's camera art.

Professor Kennedy's purpose was to provide museums, art students, and scholars in America with an authoritative photographic record of the magnificent Renaissance sculpture to be found in the palaces, churches, and shrines of Tuscany. Assisting in this painstaking and devoted labor, Fritz Henle served an arduous and thorough apprenticeship.

Kennedy would request permission of the authorities to take photographs. When it was granted, they would erect scaffolding onto which they hoisted the large specially-constructed cameras, heavy film holders, awkward tripods, and an ingenious contrivance which furnished a movable beam of light. The photographs were made by leaving the shutter open for a long period, while Henle, crouching on the scaffolding, played a beam of light back and forth upon the subject, literally painting it with illumination.

It sometimes seemed to the young apprentice that the figures they were to photograph were always hidden in the most inaccessible niches. Often this was true; the sculpture had been so hard to reach that some of it had been seen by scholars only at a distance, and numerous errors of attribution had thus been made, which Kennedy's photographs helped to correct.

Week ends brought release from the work assignments, and left Henle free to work with his beloved Rollei. It was the antithesis of the great cameras on the scaffolds, with its extreme flexibility and the speed with which it could be brought into action. The little camera slung around his neck offered no obstruction to the free play of the photographer's creative imagination, or to the capturing of natural and spontaneous grace in his subjects. He carried it concealed under his jacket to make the forbidden picture of the interior of St. Peter's which appears on page 48.

Afoot and on bicycle, he roamed the Italian countryside, photographing the arching stone bridges, sturdy old farm houses, and lovely, obscure little churches. At the same time, he became interested in the problem of reflection, and discovered the paradox that a subject reflected in rippling water might be treated more effectively than if it were photographed directly. The picture of St. Peter's dome reflected in a puddle, on page 47, illustrates the remarkable application of this idea.

It was during this fruitful Italian period that he learned the precision which is vitally necessary in darkroom work: every article must be laid out in proper order, as though a blind man were to do the work, and the darkroom must be as spotless and dust-free as a biological laboratory. To this day, Henle prefers to do his processing in a darkroom patterned, for all its stainless steel equipment, after the ingenious one fashioned by Professor Kennedy in the barn of an Italian farm.

Fritz Henle remained in Florence until 1933, when his roving spirit began to reassert itself. The next three years saw him three times in the Near East, in Spain, and in North Africa. He visited an old school friend in India and was able to photograph that country not as a tourist, but with the sympathy which comes from close acquaintance with the people and their problems. Here too he found the Rolleiflex indispensable, because of its inconspicuousness and the absence of the self-consciousness which a larger camera invariably inspires in a subject.

In 1935 he made his first trips to Japan and China, for various transportation companies, and returned with the powerfully contrasting pair of pictures on pages 102 and 103. His first travel documentary volume, *This Is Japan*, was published after he had left Germany for the last time, the atmosphere there having grown heavily oppressive.

Fritz Henle arrived in the United States in 1936, bringing with him little baggage. His professional equipment consisted of two Rolleis and one $2\frac{1}{4}$ x $3\frac{1}{4}$ camera, which he then used for color work. (Since the introduction of Ansco's 120 color film in 1945, he has used the Rollei for color as well.)

The middle thirties saw great growth and change in photography. Two of the most important factors in its development were the rise of the picture magazine and the influence of Europeans recently arrived in this country: Munkacsi, Eisenstaedt, Goro, and Feininger. The idea of the picture-story grew, to fulfill the public's desire for dynamic journalism and the visualization of current events. Travel pictures were still largely limited to the *National Geographic Magazine* and travel folders.

Herbert Matter, a Swiss designer and photographer, invited the newly-arrived Henle to use his darkroom. Henle's earliest assignments were mostly for illustrations, such as those used with *Fortune's* story on Japan.

Henle decided to use all his available time in getting acquainted with his new country. Into an old car he put a few road maps and a good supply of film. With his Rolleis beside him, he started South. His only definite assignment was from a private health foundation, to show the living conditions of the coal miners of West Virginia. He has never forgotten how astonished and shaken he was by the discovery of the extreme poverty and desolation of certain sections of the South. He went on to New Orleans, and from there to Mexico, where he found, in the town of Taxco, an architectural backdrop that might have been transferred almost directly from the Italy he knew so well.

This was the first of countless trips during which he has crisscrossed the continent by every means of transportation. His pictures reflect the face of America, on every social level and in every section.

When he returned to New York in 1937, he became a contract photographer for *Life* magazine. The Rolleiflex made possible the kind of on-the-spot picture reporting the editors desired and aided the growth of the picture story. Adventurous imagination on the part of picture editors encouraged photographers to work out their own ideas on story assignments.

Fritz Henle's *Life* stories are many. His Texas High School story has received wide acclaim as a fine example of photo-reportage, an entirely unsensational, candid account with uncommon appeal and fine composition.

He traveled widely for *Life*, visiting England at the time of the coronation of George VI, and France just before the outbreak of World War II. It was during this trip, in 1938, that he made the pictures afterwards published in his book on Paris. He was given a great many assignments in Hollywood because of the pleasant naturalness with which he interpreted the fresh beauty of the starlets. Story specifications were becoming so exacting, however, that he began to feel restricted by them, and the old urge for preservation of absolute integrity began to make itself felt.

Back at work in New York, he photographed one of the earliest outdoor fashion stories. It was taken in the country, and entirely unposed. His unorthodox approach was appealing, and he was given more and more fashion stories until, perhaps inevitably, he became typed as a "fashion expert."

Nineteen-forty found him working for *Harpers Bazaar*. Up to that time, most fashion photography had been done with large studio cameras, but the editors of the *Bazaar* were quick to appreciate the advantages offered by the speed and flexibility of the Rollei. They liked the idea of a model presented as though in natural motion. From the beginning, Henle worked mostly out of doors. He never poses his model, or says, "Smile, dear," or suggests a posture, a gesture, or a turn of the head. He requires that his models be endowed with imagination and intelligence, in addition to the professional requisites of good looks and poise.

Fashion photography is one of the fields in which Henle's passion for naturalism has been given fullest play. He has frequently journeyed with his models to the farthest corners of this country, and to Hawaii, the Virgin Islands, Mexico, and Scotland in order to provide a background consonant with the wardrobe he has been given to photograph.

Naturalistic lighting is a further contribution to Henle's success in fashion work. He never uses photoflash to supplement sunlight, though he may employ a natural reflector, such as a beach or a white wall, to project necessary light into deep shadows.

Henle feels that there is a subtle fallacy in much of today's fashion photography: the beauty of the model is unduly emphasized, and the woman coming upon the picture in a magazine is unable to identify herself with the person wearing the garment—a process which is vitally necessary if a sale is to be effected. He feels that his naturalism promotes that sense of identification between the model and the average woman.

His use of light, which contributes so much to Henle's fashion photography, has applications in every other phase of his work. His abhorrence of artificial light, whenever it can possibly be avoided, has led to a general acceptance of the use of natural light sources among other photographers, who for many years had scarcely taken a picture without either flash or flood.

This is not to say that Henle never uses artificial light sources; he employs them whenever they can heighten the natural effect he wishes to convey. When photographing the Don Cossack Chorus in his studio, for example, he provided lighting effects which simulated those of the stage on which the Chorus would normally perform. In the photograph of Canada Lee, he used spotlights to underline the tension of the actor's powerful portrayal.

New lands and new faces continue to inspire Fritz Henle. His travel books —*Mexico, Hawaii, Paris,* and *Virgin Islands*—are conceived and executed in a pattern similar to that of the documentary motion picture. They clearly transcend mere "travel picture books" and indicate to the amateur what can be done in the way of assembling a really valuable photo record of his travels, rather than the hodge-podge of meaningless trivia too often produced by the tourist. In gathering material for these books, Henle has carefully avoided the sensational, steering clear of slums and underdeveloped areas, while at the same time he has not neglected any significant aspect of the places he depicts.

Industrial photography has demanded more and more of his time in recent years. He has done a masterful series of pictures for the Cities Service Corporation and covered the plants and processes of United States Steel. On these assignments, he does not limit himself to a bare representation of factories and machines; he endeavors to show the flow of production, from raw material to finished product, with the drama and human interest inherent in each phase of the operation. In this field, Henle has found some of his most challenging material and achieved some of his most satisfying results. The picture on page 40 is characteristic of his success in industrial photography.

Henle concedes that some of his most dramatically effective pictures have been a matter of luck. Typical of this element of chance is the striking photograph of forked lightning on page 80. But he is quick to point out that unless there is vision and thorough understanding of the medium on the part of the photographer, the best of luck will not assure real success.

An interesting and consistent element in Henle's camera work—whether fashion, figure study, or industrial, indoor or outdoor—is his use of the foreground to add interest and meaning to a subject which might otherwise be dull or prosaic. In the photograph on page 73, the limb of a dead tree, near the camera, lends interest to a picture which without it might be only a bare and ordinary photograph of the Grand Canyon. Again, on page 70, one of his Cities Service series, the powerful diagonal lines of the great swamp tree conduct the eye to the center of interest, which actually occupies only a small part of the picture area.

The challenge of interior photography without auxiliary light sources, and Henle's response to it, is convincingly demonstrated in the Paris night club setting on page 37, as well as in the two circus pictures on pages 86 and 87. In the former, the only source of light was a few flickering candles, and Henle admits that he took a chance on the success of such an exposure. In the case of the "big top" photographs, it was imperative that no accessory light be employed, for it would have destroyed the unifying effect of the spotlights which pick out the performers.

Adverse weather conditions present Henle with no problem; actually they provide him with unmatched opportunities. After a rain, there are the puddles and wet pavements which he employs so effectively for the reflections they afford. In addition to the photo of St. Peter's, which has already been mentioned, those of Mexico City Cathedral and Munich, on pages 85 and 39, demonstrate his effective use of this technique.

The picture which appears first in this volume, the negative of which is used on the jacket, shows the result of Henle's making fullest use of existing light in night photography. The whole atmosphere of the Italian street festival is conveyed, for he has allowed the patterned festoons of light to tell their own story.

Moving lights, drawing their pattern on the film, have further broadened Henle's photographic horizons. He first used this technique in night work while still a student, in 1931. The Munich picture on page 39 dates from that period. More recently, he has produced highly original results in photographing midtown Manhattan's lights from a skyscraper. With the shutter open, he rotated the camera in a vertical or horizontal plane, creating the bizarre images reproduced on page 84. He does not consider these photographs "experimental," for he was quite sure what his result would be. If they must be categorized, he says, they could be termed expressionistic.

On another occasion, in the United States Steel Plant in Gary, Ind., he used a long exposure to permit the shower of sparks from a saw to trace its image on the negative.

Fritz Henle seldom makes a formal portrait; he feels that a carefully posed photograph of the human face too often tells only part of the story, and lacks a basic element of truth. He prefers informal portraiture, which allows full play both to the subject and the photographer. Commissioned to do a portrait, he will spend hours—or days, if necessary—in acquainting himself with the habits and mannerisms and idiosyncrasies of his subject. Then, with his camera in hand, he watches for these characteristics which distinguish his subject from all others, and makes his exposure.

Diligently, Henle establishes a human-to-human contact with his subject, which he knows will overcome the natural distrust of the camera. In order to communicate fully a feeling of naturalness, he himself must be interesting to his subject.

Under ideal conditions, Henle prefers to use his Rollei hand-held for portraiture, with a shutter speed as rapid as is feasible. Occasionally, for the effect of an extreme close-up, he makes use of the Rolleinar lenses.

The portrait of Marian Anderson on page 93 achieves a strong contrast to the usual studies of her, which endow her with an almost forbidding dignity. Similarly, Henle's study of Katharine Cornell presents her in a relaxed, carefree mood. These pictures are not "candid" in the sense that they were stolen, with the subject unaware of the presence of the camera. Rather, they are candid in the real sense of the word; they speak eloquently, and they speak the truth.

### A Note on the Photographic Essay

The essay in photographic form is a modern kind of story without words, embodying elements of the narrative and of the expository. It does not attempt to record simply a given condition at a given moment, but strives to present a full story, complete in all its basic elements. Conceivably, a single picture could constitute a photographic essay, but nearly always it consists of a series of pictures.

In the group of pictures comprising Fritz Henle's essay on Georges Braque, one of the greatest of living French painters, the photographer has conveyed through the medium of his Rollei the beautiful, unpostured dignity of a man of deep feeling and splendid intellect. The place in which Braque works and lives is entirely free of artiness and show. It has the same atmosphere of simplicity and unadorned spareness we find in his paintings.

It is gratifying to discover that his paintings represent the shapes and forms which surround him in his daily life. His admiration for the art forms of antiquity is projected in modern terms. Henle does not burden us with extraneous matter; he does not photograph every inch of Braque's studio in an effort to produce a minutely-detailed and precise account of the artist's life. Much is left to the viewer's imagination. Henle lays bare the essential Braque in a few succinct pictorial statements.

The quality of the photographic essay depends, like that of the literary essay, upon the skill, taste, and discernment of its creator. It fulfills the photographer's intention in direct proportion to the degree of interest he can stimulate about his subject, the nature of the information he has to convey, and his success in projecting his own responses.

FESTIVAL ON MULBERRY STREET

SOLITUDE

SUNDAY MORNING

BROOKLYN BRIDGE

THE EMPIRE STATE BUILDING

CENTRAL PARK SOUTH

*Following pages:*

CONCIERGE OF MONTMARTRE
BOWERY, WINTER AFTERNOON

NO CHARGE FOR ADMISSION

Following pages:

MME. NISKA
LES HALLES

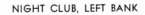

NOTRE DAME BY MOONLIGHT

ROME AT DUSK

MUNICH, RAINY NIGHT

STEEL

OIL

STRAIGHT LINES . . .

AND CURVES

REBEL IN THE MAKING

PORTUGUESE LANDOWNER

ST. PETER'S IN A PUDDLE

CAFE FLORIAN

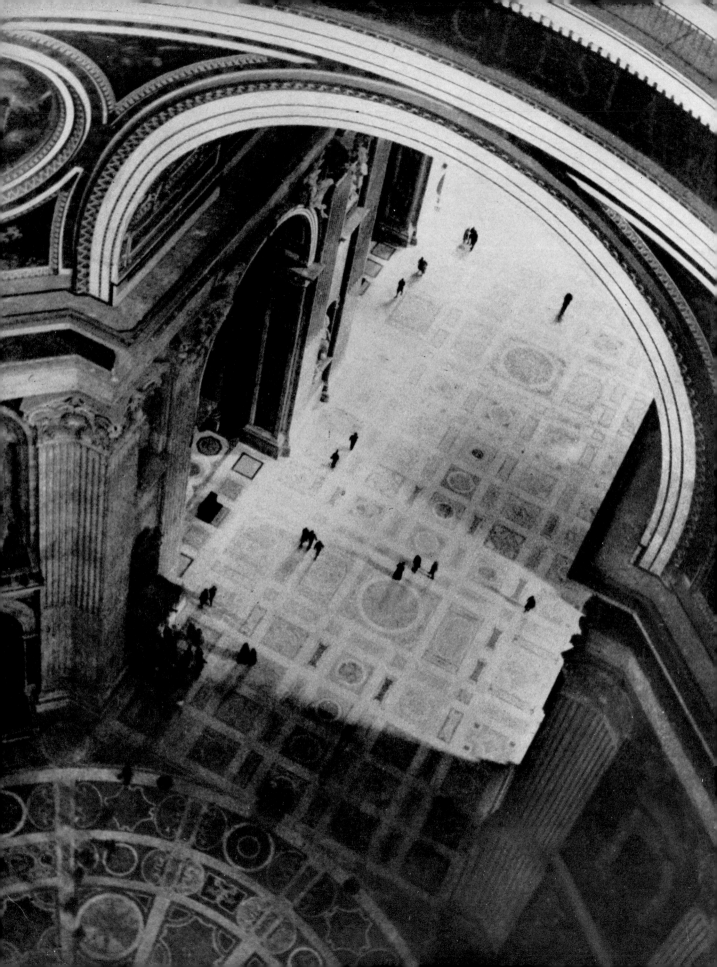

ST. PETER'S

CAMPANILE IN SIENA

LOOK UP

DRUMMER OF SIENA

CHURCH IN NORTH CAROLINA

CATHEDRAL IN ALCOBACA

MARKETPLACE, NAZARE

*Following pages:*

PORTUGUESE NETS
VERMONT BARN

THE·ORTON·FARM

MONTAUK LIGHT

BEACH AT NAZARE

BAD LANDS

MESA VERDE

TEXAS

ARIZONA

WATER'S EDGE, LOUISIANA

WATER'S EDGE, COLORADO

GRAND CANYON

DRYAD

KOA TREE

FASHION, NORTH

FASHION, SOUTH

*Following pages:* FRIEZE

THUNDERSTORM OVER TAXCO

SUNSET, TEHUANTEPEC

*Following pages:* WOMEN OF MEXICO

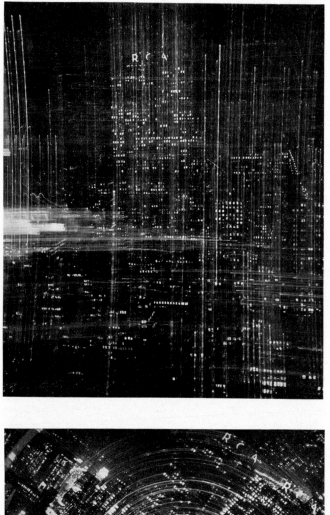

ILLUMINATIONS

AND IN THE CENTER, LADIES AND GENTLEMEN

SONG

DANCE

CANADA LEE

KATHERINE CORNELL

JOSE CLEMENTE OROZCO

DIEGO RIVERA

WOMAN REPOSING . . .

ON THE BEACH

FIGURE STUDY, POSED

FIGURE STUDY, UNPOSED

JAPAN 1935.

RUSHING WATER

SUN-SEEKER, VIRGIN ISLANDS

NET-THROWER, HAWAII

LISBON STREET SCENE

GEORGES BRAQUE

IN THE STUDIO

STILL LIFE

THE ARTIST AT WORK

# TECHNICAL DATA

**36**    **NOTRE DAME BY MOONLIGHT.** Paris, Summer 1948. Stop 5.6, 30 sec. Ansco Superpan Supreme film. D 76. Camera on tripod.

**37**    **NIGHT CLUB, LEFT BANK.** Paris, Summer 1938. Stop 3.5, 1/5 sec. Very little light available. Ansco Superpan Press film. Microdol. Camera handheld.

**38**    **ROME AT DUSK.** Summer night 1933. Stop 4, 1 minute. Agfa film. D 76. Camera on tripod.

**39**    **MUNICH, RAINY NIGHT.** Winter 1931. Stop 8, 2 minutes. Agfa film. D 76. Camera on tripod. Lights of passing cars left lighted lines on picture. My first experimental photograph.

**40**    **STEEL.** Gary Works of United States Steel Corp., July 1950. Stop 5.6, 3 sec. Very dark interior, lighted only by the millions of sparks created by the saws cutting through the still red-hot rails. Ansco Superpan Press film. Microdol. Camera on tripod.

**41**    **OIL.** Tutwiler Refinery at Lake Charles, La., 1949. Stop 5.6, 15 sec. Night. Ansco Superpan Supreme film. Microdol. Camera on tripod.

**42**    **STRAIGHT LINES.** Beach at Acapulco, Mexico, 1943. Stop 11, 1/50 sec. Superpan Supreme film. Light yellow filter. Microdol. Camera handheld.

**43**    **CURVES.** Compressor Station in Oklahoma, 1949. Stop 16, 1/25 sec. Superpan Supreme film. Light yellow filter. Microdol. Camera on tripod.

**44**    **PORTUGUESE LANDOWNER.** The Conde de Esperanza at the gate to his castle, Winter 1948. Stop 8, 1/25 sec. Rainy day. Superpan Supreme film. Light yellow filter. Microdol. Camera handheld.

**45**    **REBEL IN THE MAKING.** Tokyo high school, 1935. Stop 11, 1/50 sec. Afga film. Light yellow filter. D 76. Camera handheld.

**46**    **CAFE FLORIAN.** Venice, Summer 1933. Stop 8, 1/100 sec. Afga film. Light yellow filter. D 76. Camera handheld.

**47**    **ST. PETER'S IN A PUDDLE.** Rome, 1933. Stop 11, 1/25 sec. Bright overcast after rain. Agfa film. D 76. Camera handheld.

**48**    **ST. PETER'S.** Rome, Summer 1934. Stop 4, 1/10 sec. Agfa film, D 76. Camera handheld, bracing myself against a wall.

**50**    **CAMPANILE IN SIENA—LOOK UP.** Summer 1933. Stop 11, 1/50 sec. Agfa film. Light yellow filter. D 76. Camera handheld.

**51**    **CAMPANILE IN SIENA—LOOK DOWN.** Summer 1933. Stop 11, 1/50 sec. Agfa film. D 76. Camera handheld.

**53**    **DRUMMER OF SIENA.** Palio Festival, Summer 1933. Stop 4, 1/25 sec. Rainy day. Agfa film. D 76. Camera handheld.

**54**    **CHURCH IN NORTH CAROLINA.** Summer 1946. Stop 11, 1/50 sec. Ansco Superpan Supreme film. Microdol. Camera handheld.

55    **CATHEDRAL IN ALCOBACA.** Portugal, Winter 1948. Stop 8, I sec. Light interior. Ansco Superpan Supreme film. Microdol. Camera on tripod.

56    **PORTUGUESE WINDMILL.** Near Sintra, Winter 1948. Stop 8, 1/25 sec. Ansco Superpan Supreme film. Microdol. Light yellow filter. Camera handheld.

57    **MARKETPLACE, NAZARE.** Portugal, Winter 1948. Stop 8, 1/50 sec. Overcast day. Superpan Supreme film. Microdol. Camera handheld.

58    **PORTUGUESE NETS.** Fishermen mending their nets on the beach at Nazare. Winter 1948. Stop 16, 1/10 sec. Light overcast on beach. Ansco Superpan Supreme film. Light yellow filter. Microdol. Camera on tripod.

59    **VERMONT BARN.** Summer 1942. Stop 11, 1/50 sec. Ansco Superpan Supreme film. Light yellow filter. Microdol. Camera handheld.

60    **MONTAUK LIGHT.** Summer 1946. Stop 3.5, 2 sec. Dusk, shortly before total darkness. Ansco Superpan Supreme film. Microdol. Camera on tripod.

61    **BEACH AT NAZARE.** Portuguese fishing village, Winter 1948. Stop 16, 1/25 sec. Sun behind light overcast. Superpan Supreme film. Light yellow filter. Microdol. Camera on tripod.

62    **BAD LANDS.** New Mexico, 1941. Stop 11, 1/50 sec. Ansco Superpan Supreme film. Light yellow filter. Microdol. Camera handheld.

63    **WHITE SANDS.** New Mexico, Winter 1943. Stop 22, 1/25 sec. Ansco Superpan Supreme film. Light yellow filter. Microdol. Camera handheld.

65    **MESA VERDE.** New Mexico, Summer 1941. Stop 11, 1/50 sec. Ansco Superpan Supreme film. Light yellow filter. Microdol. Camera handheld.

66    **TEXAS.** Cowboys galloping across the plain in front of an oil rig. Summer 1949. Stop 5.6, 1/200 sec. Late afternoon. Ansco Superpan Supreme film. Microdol. Camera handheld.

67    **WILD HORSES, WYOMING.** A-A Ranch, Summer 1941. Stop 5.6, 1/250 sec. Late afternoon—against the light. Ansco Superpan Supreme film. Microdol. Camera handheld.

68    **ARIZONA.** Close-up of cactus. Stop 16, 1/25 sec. Ansco Superpan Supreme film. Microdol. Camera on tripod.

69    **ARIZONA.** Landscape. Summer 1941. Stop 8-11, 1/100 sec. Ansco Superpan Supreme film. Light yellow filter. Microdol. Camera handheld.

70    **WATER'S EDGE, LOUISIANA.** Summer 1949. Stop 16, 1/25 sec. Ansco Superpan Supreme film. Microdol. Camera on tripod.

**71**     **WATER'S EDGE, COLORADO.** Summer 1941. Stop 11, 1/50 sec. Ansco Superpan Supreme film. Light yellow filter. Microdol. Camera handheld.

**73**     **GRAND CANYON.** Summer 1941. Stop between 11 and 16, 1/25 sec. Morning light. Ansco Superpan Supreme film. Light yellow filter. Microdol. Camera on tripod.

**74**     **DRYAD.** Nude study taken in the forest, 1942. Stop 11, 1/5 sec. Bright sunny day, deep shadow effects. Ansco Superpan Supreme film. Light yellow filter. Over-exposed negative was developed only for about 5 minutes in Microdol. Camera on tripod.

**75**     **KOA TREE.** Photographed in the gardens of the Royal Hawaiian Hotel, Honolulu, Oahu, 1947. Stop 11, 1/50 sec. Late afternoon against the light for silhouette effect Ansco Superpan Supreme film. Light yellow filter. Microdol. Camera on tripod.

**76**     **FASHION, NORTH.** A McMullen dress photographed on a Long Island farm. Fall 1947. Stop 1/100 sec. Late afternoon. Ansco Superpan Supreme film. Light yellow filter. Microdol. Camera handheld.

**77**     **FASHION, SOUTH.** McMullen evening dress photographed on a Bahama beach. Spring 1947. Stop 16, 1/10 sec. Afternoon. Ansco Superpan Supreme film. Light yellow filter. Microdol. Camera on tripod.

**78**     **FRIEZE.** Women from Tehuantepec, Mexico, coming from and going to the mill. Spring 1937. Stop between 8 and 11, 1/100 sec. Noon sun. Ansco film. Light yellow filter. D 76. Camera handheld.

**80**     **THUNDERSTORM OVER TAXCO.** Summer 1943. Stop 8, 2 minutes. Photographed during a thunderstorm at night. Ansco Superpan Supreme film. Microdol. Camera on tripod.

**81**     **SUNSET, TEHUANTEPEC.** Mexico, Summer 1937. Stop 8, 1/50 sec. Ansco film. Light yellow filter. D 76. Camera handheld.

### WOMEN OF MEXICO

**82**     Old Indian woman from Taxco, 1943. Stop 11, 1/25 sec. Proxar lenses. Ansco Superpan Supreme film. Light yellow filter. Microdol. Camera handheld.

**83**     Nievis, Indian beauty and famous model of Diego Rivera. Stop 16, 1/10 sec. Ansco Superpan Supreme film. Light yellow filter. Microdol. Camera on tripod.

### ILLUMINATIONS

**84**     Radio City, Winter 1946. Stop 4, about 1 minute. Night. Ansco Superpan Press film. Microdol. Camera on tripod. By rotating tripod head the circular lines were created on the film.

**84**     Radio City, Winter 1946. Stop 4, about 1 minute. Ansco Superpan Press film. Microdol. Camera on tripod. By moving tripod slowly in horizontal and vertical directions the fine lines were imprinted on the film.

85    Mexico City Cathedral. September 1943. Stop 5.6, 10 sec. Bright illumination reflected on wet pavement after rain. Ansco Superpan Press film. Microdol. Camera on tripod.

86    **AND IN THE CENTER, LADIES AND GENTLEMEN.** The circus at Madison Square Garden, 1947. Stop 3.5, 1/5 sec. Bright spotlights concentrated on performers. Ansco Superpan Press film. Microdol. Camera handheld. Leaning firmly against my front row seat.

87    Identical with above.

88    **SONG.** Member of the Don Cossack choir photographed in the studio, 1947. Stop 8, 1/50 sec. Very bright diffused lights. Ansco Superpan Press film. Microdol. Camera handheld.

89    **DANCE.** My wife, Atti van den Berg, dancing "The Happy Maiden," 1939. Stop 5.6, 1/500 sec. Bright sunlight on outdoor stage. Very quick action. Ansco Superpan Press film. DK 20. Camera handheld.

90    **LENA HORNE.** Stop 11, one synchronized No. 2 flash bulb, 1/50 sec. Ansco Superpan Supreme film. Microdol. Camera handheld.

91    **CANADA LEE.** Studio photograph. Stop 11, 1/5 sec. two spotlights and background light. Ansco Superpan Supreme film. Microdol. Camera on tripod.

92    **KATHERINE CORNELL.** On the beach in front of her home on Martha's Vineyard, Summer 1945. Stop 11, 1/100 sec. Very bright overcast. Ansco Superpan Supreme film. Light yellow filter. Microdol. Camera handheld.

93    **MARIAN ANDERSON.** Taken in the flower garden of her farm in Connecticut, Summer 1946. Stop 8, 1/50 sec. Light yellow filter. Microdol. Camera handheld.

94    **JOSE CLEMENTE OROZCO.** Taken in Mexico City outside the church where he was painting a mural, 1943. Stop 8, 1/50 sec. Hazy day. Ansco Superpan Supreme film. Microdol. Camera handheld at low angle.

95    **DIEGO RIVERA.** He reclined next to one of his precious idols in his garden in Coyoacan, near Mexico City, Summer 1943. Stop 11, 1/25 sec. Ansco Superpan Supreme film. Microdol. Camera on tripod.

97    **WOMAN REPOSING.** Driftwood study taken at Montauk, Long Island, 1947. Stop 16, 1/25 sec. Bright diffused sunlight. Ansco Superpan Supreme film. Light yellow filter. Microdol. Camera on tripod.

99    **. . . ON THE BEACH.** Identical with above.

100   **FIGURE STUDY, POSED.** Janet Stevenson, my favorite model, posing for me on the beach at Sea Island, Fall 1947. Stop 11, 1/50 sec. Ansco Superpan Supreme film. Light yellow filter. Microdol. Camera handheld.

101 **FIGURE STUDY, UNPOSED.** My son enjoying a swim at Nantucket. Summer 1949. Stop 8, 1/100 sec. Overcast sky. Ansco Superpan Supreme film. Microdol. Camera handheld.

102 **JAPAN 1935.** A little boy at a childrens' party in Tokyo in the uniform of an admiral. Stop 11 with synchronized flashbulb at 1/50 sec. Agfa film. D 76. Camera handheld.

103 **CHINA 1935.** Young woman kissing her little son. A home in Peking. Stop 8, 1/50 sec. Agfa film. D 76. Camera handheld.

104 **RUSHING WATER.** My friend Gabriela under a refreshing waterfall in Mexico, 1943. Stop 11, 1/50 sec. Bright sunny day. Ansco Superpan Supreme film. Microdol. Camera handheld while I myself was standing waistdeep in the water.

105 **RIPPLING WATER.** Little Jan Henle, fifteen months old, trying his first swim at Nantucket Island. Stop 8, 1/100 sec. Ansco Superpan Supreme film. Light yellow filter. Microdol. Camera handheld.

105 **RIPPLING WATER.** My wife and son taking a swim at Nantucket Island, Summer 1949. Stop 8, 1/100 sec. Overcast sky. Ansco Superpan Supreme film. Microdol. Camera handheld.

106 **SUN-SEEKER, VIRGIN ISLANDS.** Photographed at Magens' Bay, St. Thomas, 1948. Stop 16, 1/10 sec. Against the late afternoon sun. Ansco Superpan Supreme film. Light yellow filter. Microdol. Camera on tripod.

107 **NET-THROWER, HAWAII.** Photographed on the island of Oahu, 1947. Stop 8, 1/250 sec. Bright sunlight at the ocean. Ansco Superpan Supreme film. Microdol. Camera handheld.

108 **LISBON STREET SCENE.** Photographed in 1949. Stop 8, 1/50 sec. Late afternoon light. Ansco Superpan Supreme film. Microdol. Camera handheld.

111 **GEORGES BRAQUE.** Summer 1948 in his Paris studio. Stop 16, 1/5 sec. Ansco Superpan Supreme film. Diffused studio light. Proxar-lenses. Microdol. Camera on tripod.

112 **IN THE STUDIO.** Stop 11, 1/5 sec. Ansco Superpan Supreme film. Diffused studio light. Microdol. Camera on tripod.

113 **CLOSE-UP.** Stop 16, 1 sec. Ansco Superpan Supreme film. Diffused sunlight. Microdol. Camera on tripod.

114 **STILL LIFE.** Stop 16, 1/2 sec. Ansco Superpan Supreme film. Diffused studio light. Microdol. Camera on tripod.

116 **THE ARTIST AT WORK.** Stop 11, 1/2 sec. Ansco Superpan Supreme film. Diffused studio light. Microdol. Camera on tripod.

117 **EXIT.** Stop 11, 1/2 sec. Ansco Superpan Supreme film. Light entrance hall. Picture taken against the light. Microdol. Camera on tripod.